FRACTIONS, DECIMALS, AND PERCENTS

by DAVID A. ADLER

illustrated by EDWARD MILLER

Holiday House / New York

COUNTY FAIR TODAY

Fractions are parts of things. **Decimals** and **percents** are parts of things too.

You can find fractions, decimals, and percents at a fair.

Cotton candy might cost 89 cents.

89 cents are part, a **fraction**, of one dollar.

There are 100 cents in one dollar.

89 cents are $\frac{89}{100}$ of one dollar.

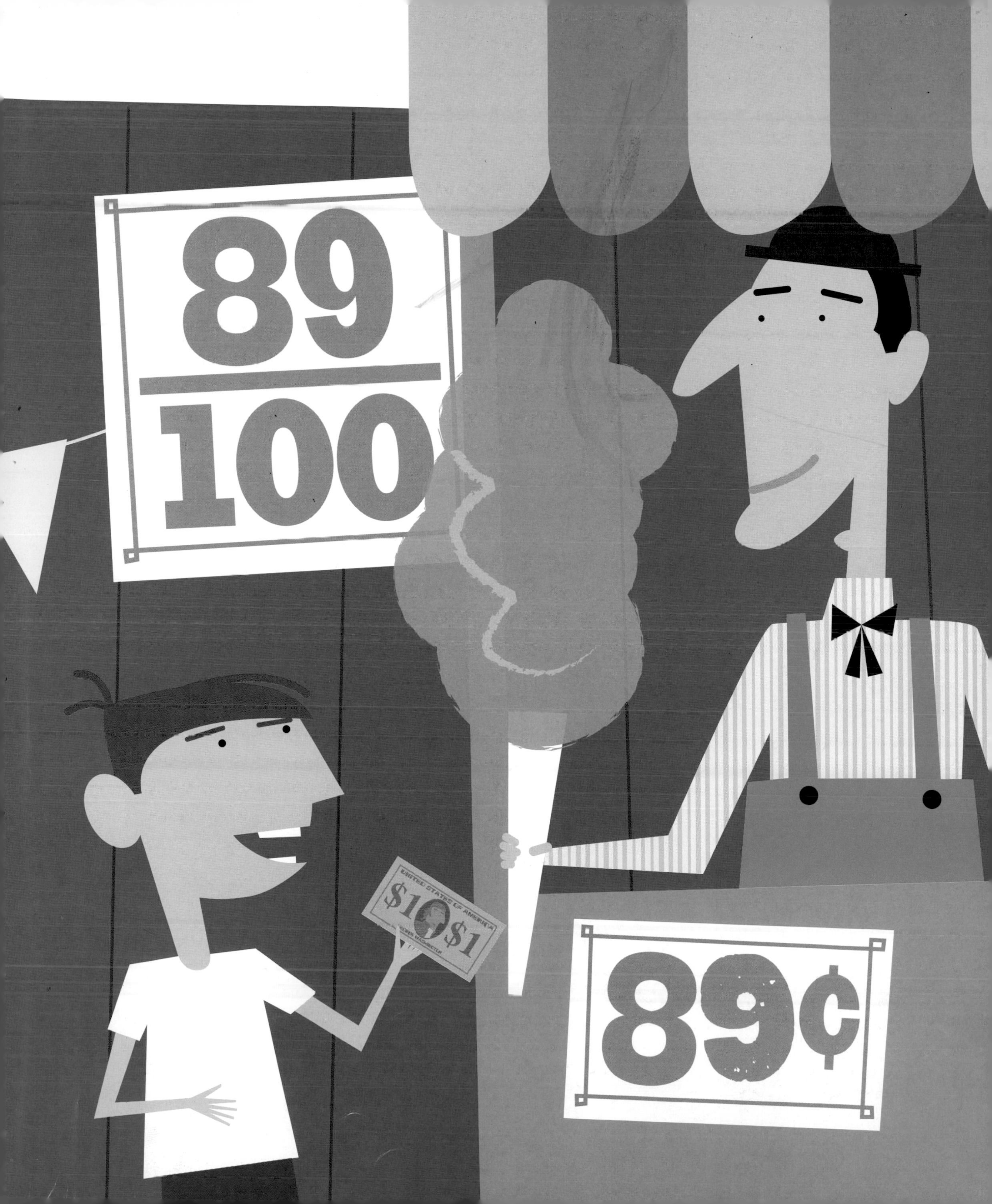
89
100
UNITED STATES OF AMERICA
$1 $1
89¢

You could also write 89 cents as $0.89. That's the cost of the cotton candy written as a **decimal**. The period (dot) before the 8 is a **decimal point**. 0.89 is the same as $\frac{89}{100}$.

You could write the cost of the cotton candy using **percent (%)**.

The cotton candy does not cost one whole dollar.

If it did, you would say it costs 100% of a dollar.

It costs less than that. It costs 89% of a dollar.

$\frac{89}{100}$, 0.89, and 89% are different ways of writing the same thing.

DONKEY RIDES

COTTON CANDY
89%
OF A DOLLAR

U.S. coins will help you understand fractions, decimals, and percents. How much money is in the box? Did you count 41 cents? You could write that as $\frac{41}{100}$, or $0.41, or 41% of a dollar.

MAGIC SHOW

$\frac{41}{100}$ OF A DOLLAR

41% OF A DOLLAR

$0.41

Count the money in this box.
Did you count 53 cents?
You could write that as $\frac{53}{100}$ of a dollar,
or $0.53, or 53% of a dollar.

$\frac{53}{100}$

$0.53

53%

Now count the money in this box.

$$\frac{??}{100} \qquad \$0.?? \qquad ?\%$$

What fraction of a dollar is in the box?

How would you write that as a decimal?

How would you write that as a percent of a dollar?

TICKET

Answers: $\frac{17}{100}$ of a dollar, $0.17, 17% of a dollar

The coins in each box were a fraction of a dollar. Now take a look at these fractions: $\frac{41}{100}$, $\frac{53}{100}$, and $\frac{17}{100}$.

The bottom number, the **denominator**, tells you how many cents there are in one dollar.

The top number, the **numerator**, tells you what part of a dollar— how many cents—you have.

Going once, going twice, sold for $999.99
$9,000.00
$999.99
1
WINNER
$900.00
AUCTION AT NOON

Now look around the fair.
You'll see lots of decimals.
A champion lamb might cost $999.99.
999.99 is a decimal.
With decimals, there is no bottom or top
number, no denominator or numerator.
Each of the 9s in 999.99 means something different.
What matters is on which side of the decimal point
the digit 9 is written and how close it is to the decimal point.
900.00, 90.00, and 9.00 are not the same.
0.90 and 0.09 are not the same.
900.00 is nine **hundreds**.
90.00 is nine **tens**.
9.00 is nine **ones**.
0.90 is 9 **tenths**, $\frac{9}{10}$.
0.09 is 9 **hundredths**, $\frac{9}{100}$.

WIN A TRIP TO THE BIG CITY WORTH
$735.46

HUNDREDS **TENS** **ONES** **TENTHS** **HUNDREDTHS**

Take a look at this diagram. It will help you understand how the value of a digit is different when it's on the right or left side of the decimal point and how close it is to the decimal point.

The 7 means 7 hundreds, or 700.

The 3 means 3 tens, or 30.

The 5 means 5 ones, or 5.

The 4 means 4 tenths, or $\frac{4}{10}$.

The 6 means 6 hundredths, or $\frac{6}{100}$.

Percent means "out of 100."
40% means the same as $\frac{40}{100}$.
It's the same as 0.40.
People often use percent when they
talk about parts of prices.
40% off the price of a toy means
it costs 40% less than 100%
of the regular price.
40% less than 100% is 60%. Instead
of $1.00, the toy would cost $0.60.

$\frac{40}{100}$ OFF

GAMES

SALE!
$0.40
OFF OF
EACH
DOLLAR!

40%
OFF

To change each of those fractions
to a decimal or a percent you **divide**.

$$\frac{1}{2} \quad \frac{3}{4} \quad \frac{4}{5} \quad \frac{NUMERATOR}{DENOMINATOR}$$

First you change the numerator
into a decimal.
1 becomes 1.00.
3 becomes 3.00.
4 becomes 4.00.

MERLYN
THE MAGNIFICENT
MATHEMATICIAN

Then you divide the numerator by the denominator.

```
      .50              .75              .80
  2)1.00          4)3.00          5)4.00
   -10↓            -28↓            -40↓
   ────            ────            ────
    00              20              00
                   -20
                   ────
                    0
```

$\frac{1}{2}$ IS THE SAME AS 0.50 AND 50%

$\frac{3}{4}$ IS THE SAME AS 0.75 AND 75%

$\frac{4}{5}$ IS THE SAME AS 0.80 AND 80%

Fractions, decimals, and percents can each be used to say something is less than one. But there are times people mostly use fractions, times people mostly use decimals, and times people mostly use percents.

PIE-EATING CONTEST

1ST PRIZE

If the man at the pie eating contest ate four full pies and half of a fifth pie, he would probably use a fraction.

He would probably say, "I ate 4 and $\frac{1}{2}$ pies."

He probably would not say, "I ate 4.5 pies."

But he could!

He probably would not say,

"I ate 4 pies and 50% of a fifth pie."

But he could!

I ATE 4.5 PIES!

Let's play baseball at the arcade.

You hit the ball 3 times out of 10 tries.

If someone asks, "What's your batting average?"

you would probably answer that question with a decimal.

You would say, "I batted .300."

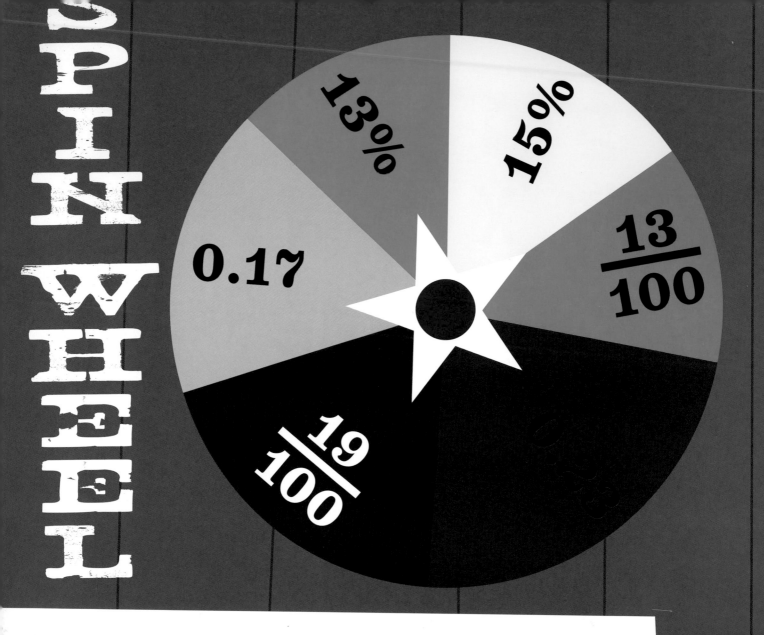

SPIN WHEEL

15%

13%

0.17

$\frac{13}{100}$

$\frac{19}{100}$

MATCHING GAME

8% 0.15 0.63 0.45 30%

0.30 45% 15% 0.08 63%

Look around the fair.

Each time you see a fraction, see if you can change it to an equivalent decimal and percent.

Each time you see a decimal, see if you can change it to an equivalent fraction and percent.

Each time you see a percent, see if you can change it to an equivalent fraction and decimal.

EXIT

1/8	0.125	12.5%
1/4	0.25	25%
3/8	0.375	37.5%
1/2	0.50	50%
5/8	0.625	62.5%
3/4	0.75	75%
7/8	0.875	87.5%

Look around when you go shopping.
You see fractions, decimals, and percents in shopping malls.
You see fractions, decimals, and percents in
sports stadiums and newspapers.
Fractions, decimals, and percents are everywhere.

100%
NATURAL

FOR
SaLe
$5.99

APPLES
50¢ FOR
$\frac{1}{4}$ LB.

$\frac{1}{2}$
PRICE
SALE

15%
OFF

SALES
TAX
8%

30.5
MILES
PER
GALLON

Salt Water Taffy
• 2 cups sugar
• 2 tablespoons cornstarch
• 1 cup light corn syrup
• ¾ cup water
• 2 tablespoons butter
• 1 teaspoon salt
• ¼ to 1 teaspoon flavoring (such as vanilla, lemon, or mint)
• 3 drops food coloring (optional)

BASEBALL STANDINGS

	W	L	Pct.
	20	10	.667
	18	11	.621
	14	16	
	13	12	
	12	17	

.286
.232
.298
.239
.083
.105

FRaCTiON, DeCiMaL, PeRCeNT MeMORY

A game for two or more players

You'll need:

- 36 index cards
- a pen, pencil, or marker

On each of 36 cards, write a different fraction, decimal, or percent.

If you wrote a fraction, write its equivalent as a decimal or a percent on another card.

If you wrote a decimal, write its equivalent as a fraction or a percent.

If you wrote a percent, write its equivalent as a fraction or a decimal. Now you are ready to play.

Mix up the cards. Turn them over and place them on a flat surface in rows.

Now take turns turning over cards, two cards at a time. If the cards match (0.51 matches 51%; $\frac{3}{100}$ matches 0.03), the player keeps the cards and goes again.

If the cards don't match, the player turns over the cards so the blank sides are showing and leaves the cards in their original positions. Now it's the next player's turn. The game ends when all the cards are taken. The player with the most cards is the winner.

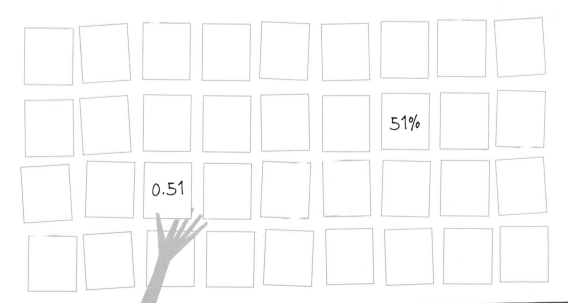

You can go to website: www.edmiller.com for cards that are ready to print and cut out.

Text copyright © 2010 by David A. Adler
Illustrations copyright © 2010 by Edward Miller III
All Rights Reserved
HOLIDAY HOUSE is registered in the U.S. Patent and Trademark Office.
Printed and Bound in October 2009
in Johor Bahru, Johor, Malaysia, at Tien Wah Press.
www.holidayhouse.com
First Edition
1 3 5 7 9 10 8 6 4 2

Library of Congress Cataloging-in-Publication Data

Adler, David A.
Fractions, decimals, and percents / by David A. Adler ;
illustrated by Edward Miller.
p. cm.
ISBN 978-0-8234-2199-2 (hardcover)
1. Fractions—Juvenile literature. 2. Decimal fractions—Juvenile
literature. 3. Percentage—Juvenile literature. I. Miller, Edward, 1964- ill.
II. Title.
QA117.A256 2010
513.2′6—dc22
2008048464

Photos of coins © 2010 by Lauren Ann Sasso

To my adorable grandson,
Jonathan "Yoni" Alex
—D. A. A.

To my friend
Lyndsey Royce
—E. M.

Visit **www.davidaadler.com** for more information on the author, for a listing of his books, and to download teacher's guides and educational materials. You can also learn more about the writing process, take fun quizzes, and read select pages from David A. Adler's books.

Visit **www.edmiller.com** for activities that accompany this book. Join the Edward Miller Fan Club to receive e-mail announcements of new books, activities, and free book contests.